I0138515

Praise for *souldust*

"In this exquisite collection of poems, Lisa O'Neil-Guerci professes the many forms of love everywhere her graceful eyes softly land. *Souldust* captures the truth held inside our longings, our grief and losses, within our connections, and in all the places we yearn to be seen. Whether it be heard in the whispering leaves and seen as sign posts along a summer walk, or in one sweeping moment watching the pouring rain, each lyrical poem offers an honest reflection and reveals the close-knit feelings we share as humans. Read this book and you will be enchanted, consoled, uplifted and understood."

—SUSAN FRYBORT, author of *Look to The Clearing, Open Passages,* and *Hope is a Traveler*

"Lisa O'Neil-Guerci's debut book of poems is filled with the soul of a mystic. She writes fresh and casts a spell of whimsy, wonder, and warmth. Lisa notices the details of our emotions. She doesn't shy away from life's questions and then delivers her wisdom. This is her gift to us. Poems of grace and intelligence bestowed with a fierce heart full of love."

—CAROLYN M. RIKER, poet & writer of *Blue Clouds* and *The Colors I Hear*

souldust

souldust

a collection
of reflections

Lisa O'Neil-Guerci

2024

GOLDEN DRAGONFLY PRESS

AMHERST, MASSACHUSETTS

FIRST PRINT EDITION, April 2024
FIRST EBOOK EDITION, April 2024

Copyright © 2024 by Lisa O'Neil-Guerci.
Cover Art by Beth Hannis.
All rights reserved.

No part of this publication may be reproduced or transmitted in any form
or by any means, electronic or otherwise, without prior written permission
by the copyright owner.

ISBN: 979–8–9894116–1–0

Library of Congress Control Number: Requested

Printed on acid-free paper supplied by a Forest Stewardship Council-certified
provider. First published in the United States of America by Golden Dragonfly
Press, 2024.

www.goldendragonflypress.com

Dedicated to my brilliant children:

Lea, full of stars in her eyes
and the childlike wonder of a night sky,
and Andrew; the wise, kind man in the moon,
yet grounded to the earth.

They have taught me the lessons of unconditional love.

Contents

Introduction

D o you sometimes feel as if life has ground you to powder, or smashed your last dream? Do you question the meaning of existence in the grand scheme? Do you ever see yourself as an insignificant mote of dust in the midst of a windstorm? Have you ever searched for answers in a cloud's changing shape, the ocean mist kissing your face, or in the lessons learned from longing, love, and loss?

In this debut collection of poetry and prose, I invite you into my way of looking at the world; through a lens of wonder and enchantment, in which particles of feelings and experiences shimmer and swirl in sunbeams and on cloudy days.

Through each of these poems, I channel the Muse through the magic I notice in Nature, in the unique details of each season, as I explore beauty in all its mysterious forms.

Join me on this journey as I travel from trauma to triumph, as I discover and uncover awe in the world that surrounds us, as well as the deeper one within.

Listen with me to the clarity found in the voice of soundless woods, in the quiet flight of birds, and in the myriad miracles that walk across the lake on which I live.

I wrote this book to be a kind of roadmap, a compass, a blueprint with which to create a rich appreciation of life's many blessings, a guide to being a divinely inspired human with feet planted firmly on the yielding earth.

May these verses elicit a nod of empathy, a sense of recognition and familiarity, and a shared conviction that there is a vast knowingness to the ever-evolving, benevolent Universe which reaches far beyond what our five senses perceive as "real."

Let these words soothe your troubled heart and mind, as they illustrate that, more than mere vessels of clay, we are cannons containing glorious confetti.

We are made of *Souldust*.

Souldust

Souldust isn't just the ash
remaining
when one departs

or what whirls up like a dervish
from a pile of amber leaves
after burning.

It's in the whorls of dustbowl dreams
and discarded memories

it's the sheer powder layer
on the wing of a moth

bleached shells crushed
beneath the feet of time

the glittering particles
suspended
in beams of sunlight
streaming into a life

what shimmers in shafts
of moonlight
when the glow dissolves
into the dance of fairies.

Souldust isn't decay.
It is that which breathes life
into new creation;

what's strewn into the air
when exhaled from the soul

to see where the wind will take it…

Island

It's understandable—

this putting up of walls
built in the space
between us.

they are erected
for protection,
inclusion,
exclusion.

There is less pain
on a lonely island,
yet
the aching
throb of frustration
asserts itself

a mirage of echoes
and faux rescues.

Sometimes
I'm willing to debride
the clutter of
thinking
to just imagine
there are others with me
in the wondrous
indolence
of this afternoon.

The air wants to be shared.
It's
ripe with the scent of rain
which fell
just moments ago.

The space between us,
a desert,
then a voice.

Words
evoke an oasis
in the midst
of arid indifference

and poetry
always
opens
windows.

Windchime Mind

My mind
is a wind chime
twirling and tangled
in the chaos of
a hurricane.

How I long for it
rather to be
like a leaf or petal
falling softly
from flower or tree

floating down quietly
to other thoughts
and hundreds of tears
drifting downstream.

Breeze and Shade

I waited
in the stifling heat,
and heard a rustling—
felt a slight breeze.
Tree trunks in clumps,
standing like companions.

At first glance, indistinguishable as separate,
yet sharing one purpose, one voice.
Vines creep up—
the ropey kudzu thick,
while roots beneath
remain unseen
entwined underground,
earth-bound lovers
engaged in lusty coupling.

Or are these aged trunks brothers,
soldiers huddled together,
stronger when united?

It brings my heart a strange sweet joy,
to see this sturdy base for one huge tree
boasting the grandest green umbrella
I have ever seen

its mighty arms of bark
praising the sun,
its tender leaf hands praying,
playing with the sky.

Seek the Light

Seek the light
even in that
porous heart of yours
when and where
it might not seem
particularly
bright.

Seek the light.

See it sparkling through trees,
becoming leafless now.
See how it shines on the red-orange sisal
of the earth's floor.

Seek the light that peeks out behind clouds
in the sky of your mind.

Seek it in conversations
with the weary
who need to see
the comforting lighthouse beacon
of your words.

Seek the light
when you feel like a thunderstorm
that remembers rainbows.

Seek the light
in your soul.

Let it infuse,
surround,
suffuse
your presence.

Be that candle in the window
dancing eternally.

Seek the light
still present
in the eyes of the suffering
and the dying,
and in what still blesses
the crumpled fauna of Fall
on the ground.

Seek the light
in each gentle sunrise
and in the colors of every sunset,

and don't forget
the luminescence of
the gently glowing moon.

Seek the light
in the gray rain
of your life.

It is always there:
the Universe's light bulb,
a flashlight when you're lost,
a nightlight when you're lonely
and sleep is elusive.

Seek the light.

The light is seeking you.

A Day Unmet

A fence,
a stone wall,
this velvet
bit of moss
that greets my bare feet.

Kiss of warm breeze,
sun shimmering
behind clouds
indulging in sky:

the blue,
the green,
the white
of milkweeds' hair.

Bird and brook
conspire together…
a most beautiful duet

beckoning me forward
ever deeper,

into a day
I've never met.

A Book Unfolding

As a youth,
trapped,

I hung out,
hid out

in the library—

a sacred space,
a hold-fast,
a sanctuary.

I often retreated to a treehouse, too.
There, leaves of imagination grew,
in a place where no hands could reach me.

I can still smell the leather and wood
of the rooms
where I was happy to read anything new,
as well as Alcott,
Herriot,
Tolkien,
and Blume.

Where quiet contentment
was assured,
and all I heard
were pages turning,
or the soft scratching
of writing implement
to hungry paper.

There,
in secure fortress,
I wrote
the story of my unusual life.

Words were then
and still are
my armor,
a sword traded
for the mightier quill.

In a childhood where I was held hostage
by false gods
and evil men,

I decided that my exodus
would flow through ink.
My future would unfold
with the power
of a pen.

And through my own words—
not his,
not theirs,
I'd make it to heaven.

I escaped
to a vast, celestial
library—

but not for a moment loftier
than my five senses allowed.

For me,
you see,

the specter
of eternity
is just to rest a mind

wearied
by mere mortality—

too brief to read
all the words,
all the books,
all the poems.

And I want
to write prose
as well;
in various tongues
of expression.

The margins are
where I get to define
a subtle divide
between a hellish adolescence
and what is divine.

At last, my mind quieted
to summon the muse:

a holy
ghost-writer
named creativity

written in calligraphy;
gracefully looping letters
in the shape of a sideways number eight
indicating
Infinity.

The Gift of Spring

I can't wait
to walk around the lake
and see what is happening now—
to take a lingering look around

at what is opening
and awakening
from the thawing ground;

the sleepy eyes of budding growth
and tendril arms
stretching towards sun
leaning into
the gentle caress of warmer air.

I can't wait
to notice
the way birdsong is different now,
how the notes float higher,
in lighter air, somehow.

I can't wait
to be humbled
before the new season,
privileged to be
a witness to Spring—

though the earth and its creatures
have carried it within all along,

bursting like children holding secrets
they can't wait
to disclose.

Spring knows, in its silence,
how resolute
and absolute
are the colors of grace.

And so I walk this prayer
as my feet
thank the spongy soil
and clean fresh air

my heart
filled with gratitude
to fertile Goddess,
for the perennial gift
of new life.

Hope

It is a time of bewildering darkness.
Yet there they are,

small favors from a vast,
benevolent universe:

flowers in a cobalt vase,
a slender shaft of sunlight
filtered through
the attic window

just above a sheltering roof.

Sustenance enough is found there;

a friend with whom to share
a simple meal
and a feast
of memories
tucked into yellowed scrapbooks.

The future may be
a fog of uncertainty
as it ever has been,

yet it remains intact
in the eyes of children
who awaken
from nightmares
to find comfort

in the arms of those who hold hope
close to their unguarded hearts

and refuse to let go.

Mitchell and Me

There is no melancholy
more voluptuous,
than this sultry evening,

sitting on my front steps
with my cigarette

listening
to the songs of crickets
lake peepers,
and Joni.

There is no feeling more poignant
at this moment.

But I have learned
as long as I've lived
that there will be another moment.

Then another.

And I might change my mind
and mood
many times between moments
between songs

before that rogue coyote comes
along.

He was last seen
on track one…

I'm as solo as she
when she was
traveling traveling traveling
when she soaked those long dry roads
with liquid lyrics:
her blood and sweat,
her wine and tears—

crafting yet another songbook
from all she saw, felt,
and met throughout the years

from all whom she
loved,
lost
lusted after,
and learned from.

Suddenly,
I am filled
with a certain ennui
and then an immediate
buoyancy
each time I hear the evocative
opening chords
of Coyote.

For right now, though,
for my mood,
I need *Hejira*
to surround and
suffuse me.

So I close my eyes,
tilt my head back,

inhale the sound,
and luxuriate
in this tender ache,

then exhale smoky
tendrils;
like her
"white flags from winter chimneys
waving truce
against the moon."

God,
how I love that evocative line.

Joni,
you can sit on my steps,
share a smoke,
and sing to me

anytime.

Wounded Healer

Is your heart broken?
Share from it, still.

Is it cracked wide open
because it lay precariously
upon a fault line
of feeling?

Let sweet searching souls,
soldiers
reach inside
with both hands,
elbows-deep
to clean the wound,
to solder
and suture.

And then,
when your heart is mended,
tender again,
and able to bear
weight,
let it overflow
as a cornucopia does…

or an egg,
spilling out its moonlight white
and sunshine yolk
to nourish
the hungry others.

For when that which pulses heartily
after having echoed
with vacant loneliness
for so long
in the holy hollow
of past years
opens up
again—

there's ample room
for others to crawl inside,
to sit with you
in warm rooms
and soothing chambers
and steady and sanguine

sharing the whoosh and return
as your heart
fills up—

over and over.

Again and again.

Poetry Is a Family

Poetry is a family, a recognized tribe.

Words meet up
at functions,
weddings,
reunions,
celebrations,
funerals
where
we gather

to eat,
to laugh,
to savor.

Poetry is a family—
a picnic,
with baskets overflowing,

with words to eat,
to drink,
to reminisce,
at a table, groaning.

Where we smile,
hug,
cry,
and kiss.

Poetry is a family,
Words that weep familiar tears,

the wry smile
of the recognized,
the confessions,
and the fears.

The nodding
nostalgia,
and secrets held within hearts,
then shared.

Poetry is a family:
phrases as cousins,
uncles and aunts,
weaving stories
in ancestral language,

a scrapbook of
history filling uncountable pages.

Poetry contains
future plans
and memory's mystery—

no scapegoats here,
or once cast aside
black sheep.

The affection at this reunion is real,
feelings are so deep.

Thicker than blood,
words flow like water.

Poetry is a family:

mother,
father,
son, and
daughter.

Blessing

I only had to rearrange a bit,

make room for it,
leave the door ajar.

I only needed to step aside,
call off the search,
the begging insistence
that it bends to my will.

I only needed to be still.

I couldn't call into existence
what was there all along
unhidden,
unbidden—
an unsung song.

I opened the door a little wider.
Ah, there you are,
Blessing.

I'm sorry I kept you waiting.

Welcome home.

Living Mandala

She is a living mandala,
my first child,
my only daughter,
now grown.

She has blossomed since birth,
more vibrant each year,
since that November night
when she exploded into this world
Like supercharged fireflies
amidst fireworks,
showering the air around her
and the ground
with the brightest of crackling lights.

I see her now
living her life,
ever unfurling
like a tapestry to be hung
proudly,
gracefully
on the smooth wall
of each new day.

She is a living mandala
formed of petals and peace,
mystery and intent—

a windmill
in perpetual motion,
painted with wildflowers

and surrounded by the heartbeats
that budded inside her
then magnified out:

the first child
whose smile is hers.
The second,
fiercely himself
created,
curated
with her *Anam Cara*
best friend love.

She is a living mandala:
all swoops and swerves
and gently sloping curves—

a swirling spiral
easing gently inward,
then back out again…
reaching.

Slender arms
with small,
adept hands
always tender enough to hold
protectively,
affectionately
her loves
and fierce enough
to shatter to dust—
all that might foolishly dare
to impede her path.

Now those hands and arms
undulate upwards
to embrace
the air—
all that it contains
and all it brings forth
as new life.

Two sons now.
Two golden chalices.

He Is in the Garden with Me

Elegant swans
and ducks that waddle,
chuckling as they eat
flowers blooming boldly,
songbirds,
and tiny sparrows so sweet.

The lake
mirrors the clouds.

The warm massage of sunshine,
and rushing water
so loud

with the fertile growth
of all that is green
surrounding me.

How can I question Gaia's ebullient
beauty?

As I sit in my garden
delighted
and awed

how can I question
the presence of God?

Empathy

And what a thing

it would be
if one day
we realized
the truth of empathy—that each one of us
is blind in some way.

We would guide each other home,
we would help each other see.

We'd gently reach through
to read the Braille
written on each and every soul.

We'd trace one another's truth
with an exquisitely tender touch—
with sensitive fingertips.

We would be each other's sharpened senses.

We would be each other's eyes.

When Mary Oliver Passed

Where are you this morning, Mary?

Dawn found me standing
at the edge of the lake
slushy with February's reluctant thaw.

The wild geese were there,
of course.

As I endeavored to view
my life
through a zen
lens,
attempting
not to alter people
or circumstances
by the way I see them,

it occurred to me:
there are no answers.
Not really.
There is only the sitting still,
the process of pondering
and prayer,
the journey
and those concepts
I made complicated
so damn long.

There is only one energy,
one life

wild and precious.
You queried:
"What do you plan to do with it?"

Dearest Muse,
I have so many plans
and
frustrated dreams
and often feel paralyzed and inept

"Well, what do you want?
what do you have?"
I envision you asking.

I have this life,
this day.

I have the smiles of my children
and grandsons swiftly growing
into all their innate curiosity
and questions, too.

I have this cup of coffee
clutched in my still-sleepy hand.

I have the lyrical gift of Joni
on constant shuffle.

I have two
velveteen cats,
indolent and fat,
who show me daily
how to lazily lounge around
on the sunny windowsill of life,

how to close my eyes
and purr.

I have poetry to read
and write.
It is my inspiration,
respiration,
and respite;
my pulse,
my fiercest passion.

and nature
which gives to all
and asks no questions.

Birds and flowers never insist
upon themselves,
as we foolish humans are wont to do.
They simply
are.

Mary,
when you transitioned
to the other side,
it was as if the cornucopia of your mind
and heart
fell off a stone wall
cut through with the softest moss
and spilled out.

And I am a hungry young bird,
digesting your every word

I have the gifts of interest
and inner
adventure.

May I share these gifts
as freely as you did,
and still do,
for poetry is eternal.

So again I ask you, Mary,
Where are you flying off to?

Is your place
in the V-formation
of the wild geese aloft?

Maybe you're meandering
on the edge of a marsh,
your feet sinking into the ground
boggy and so soft.

Or perhaps sitting on a rock,
somewhere in the Great Beyond,
scribbling in the
little notebook
you carried,
as you took a walk to the pond—

All the while smiling your sly grin
as the morning mist kisses you awake.

Full Moon Calling

There is a full moon tonight
rising
like God's best idea

glowing,

speaking to me in her silence.

Something restless in me responds,
growling,
hungry.

Is it the wolf in me, stirring?

I do feel stirred of late…
moved,
restive,
inspired to create—

to express
all that has been hiding
without reason
in a cave of my deepest self
for the longest season.

The air
warmed by spring
calls me
from my lair.

Now I prowl
through unknown territories,
but are they really unknown?

I'm stalking my dreams
which know my name,
time to stake claim
to hunt what is mine—

to move silent as a tomb,
my compass,
the light of the moon.

It's time to lean my head back,
to be fearless to the night

time at last to sound out my haunting howl.

All that is alive and keening
this evening
bids me to join in.

My eyes
stare back
at the moon's icy glare
glowing with fire.

Luna is no longer beyond reach,
though it rises ever higher.

Farewell to My Father

That day came
in 1980.

I kept a diary,
even then.

The entry read:
"Early this morning,
Daddy died."

How inexplicable,
how shocking
is death
to a 13-year-old girl
just learning about life?

I wonder now:
why.
when.
how.

I discarded that little journal
with its heart-shaped lock
and stashed-away
tiny skeleton key
I found so precious,
so charming.

Did I think that
by no longer journaling,

it would erase what that night
did to me?
How it forever affected me?

Can words once written,
ever really be thrown away?
The pain stays.
Words remain.
Indelible ink.
A lifelong stain.

I find it amazing
that I had
the mental
and emotional wherewithal
to write that morning,
anything at all—

to construct a five word sentence
succinct
and concise.

Words spilled like tears
onto that neatly-lined page
in black ink
as sharp as death,
the start of my stifled rage.

It's amazing how writing was
always something in which
I tucked myself away—
a closet where one keeps things
folded up,
neat,
and safe:

big secrets,
dreams,
pre-adolescent tragedies,
and all that was
before
That Day...

simple
and sweet.

I later wrote of that night,
the furtive, futile prayers
when the phone rang
at a peculiar
hour.

Phones don't tend to ring
late at night
unless something is wrong.
Very wrong.
Nothing could make this right.

An uncle had come.
my mother's brother—
tall and warm and comforting.

I remember his
strong,
sad,
presence,
terribly troubled.

My father too

had been tall,
strong in his way—
A big gentle bear
to me.

I remember as a child,
(when I still was one),
standing behind him
to wrap my arms
around his belly.

And that night
was the last time I saw him.

Alive,
anyway.

Then a white rose,
my tiny white bible.
I felt both soothed,
and betrayed
by God,
a Being I thought I knew…

but, back then,
in very strange ways…

Clutching that book
to my chest,
my heart beating like a rabbit's,
when trapped
was just something I thought
I should do
to remain somewhat intact.

My brother,

still asleep,
but I already knew:
they wanted to wait
till he woke
to tell him
the nightmare news.

Oh, how unbearable
that
daybreak was.

Broken too, was
the very air I breathed,
filled with silent shrieking
and the sound
of shattered glass.

I greeted the dawn with grief;
tangled,
jumbled,
mangled.

Then the muffled,
mumbled,
vague apologies.

But what, really, can one say?
What words can spirit
reality
away?

And I knew,
deep within,
that I'd have to fast-forward,

I'd have to grow,
even while being paralyzed
in that time—

a complex knot of roots
beneath the surface
of that moment,
petrified.

And the unexpected
would come to be
what was inexplicably
expected of me.

I'd learn to
raise myself—
feral,
to phoenix
though I didn't know
the meaning
of either.

What I did know
was that life
would never be the same—

not that it had been normal at all
before that day
in any way.

I heard
and felt
a steel door clanging—
thick metal
separating prison

from freedom…
That day was a brick
thrown into pastel,
chalk dust
imaginings,
a thick stick thrust
into the spokes of my world,

a coal-black
permanent marker
delineating time.

The stark, strange
unchangeable change
between yesterday
and today…

I was thirteen.
going on old.
I didn't realize then
what was to be
or become,

his thirty-eight being
impossibly young.

Aging stopped.
His and mine.

I was only thirteen
going on never,
going on forever

And as his soul
floated away
on ethereal waves,
my childhood froze in time.

Church in the Woods

I am invited to come to church today,
so I simply step outside,

and in an instant,
my heart
finds reverence
in the quiet grace

of this green space,
and then it opens wide.

No walls
are needed
when the steeple is the top
of a mighty conifer
I sit beneath.

This tree knows the gift,
the miracle,
of Christmas morning every day.

I lift my face to praise the sky,
and gaze in wonder at the stained-glass prisms
which dance in the mist over the lake,

the sun shining through the leaves
like flickering candles.

I sing in the choir of creation.
I lay the gifts of my awe and gratitude
at an altar fashioned

of tamped-down flora
of all that lived before;

the sisal of moss and branches
is the humble, holy floor,

a smooth boulder for a pew.

I hear an organ
in the humming hymn of frog and cormorant—
songs lifted to heaven
by a dragonfly's wings.

His sermon is silence.

Inspiration found in His palms
in the psalm of this season.

Leaves crunch tenderly
under my knees
as I kneel on soft ground
to pray.

Book of Life

Born as letters
then words
in a brief mysterious
life.

Lines of childhood
turn to adolescent paragraphs
until the chapters of adulthood unfold.

Now that I am older,
has the story really been told?

Perhaps someone somewhere
will hold the book of me
pressed to their chest,
close to their heart.

Maybe they will sleep with it
tucked under their pillow.

Perhaps I was a brief love poem
in another's life
or an ode to many.

When it's time
to close the book,
maybe I will be placed
gently upon a shelf
where memories keep my spine supple
so that others can flip through my pages
from time to time.

May I live so that I might be
a treasured volume
a cherished tome
to tote around.

I'd like a burnished cherry wood bookcase
to be my home,
and my dearest wish
is that my words will be tasted
in hungry mouths,
held
in tender hands

so that curious minds might find
what they didn't know they were looking for

as they browse through
the story
of my life.

Fairies

I think the world needs more fairies,
more enchantment.

We need more than a day
filled with the ordinary.
How can fairies be imaginary
when the very idea of them fills
the senses with delight?

I think the world needs more fairies
with their delicate firefly light,
more innocent astonishment
and inquiry
more awe-filled
wonder
and curiosity.

I think the world needs more fairies
to water the smallest of flowers
with kisses of dew,
to visit the gardens each morning
when dawn makes everything new,
to befriend the greedy squirrels
and field mice,
to check in with chipmunks
as big as bears to them.

I think the world needs more fairies
to flaunt and flutter
their iridescent wings
alongside hummingbirds,

dragonflies,
and crickets
with symphonies to sing.

I think the world needs more fairies
to ride upon the blue jay's back,
hail a ride from a finch's yellow cab,
and splash with abandon
with sparrows
in their concrete bath.

I think the world needs more fairies
so that we may appreciate the small things:

the overlooked,
the ignored,
the unseen.

This world needs more magic
and would have it
if fairies lived in more
than just
a child's dreams…

Song of the Crone

Aging
is a beautiful thing,
not to be set aside
in some future 'somewhere.'

Aging
is nature.

Seeds to sagacious seasons,
secrets held
in rutted hands
and the rivulets of smile lines
on the landscape
of a face that has lived,
truly lived.

Aging
is the graceful, grateful letting go,
as russet leaves do
when they fall from sturdy limbs
which have held storms
and the tiny nests of youth.

Aging
is the burnished gold of wisdom,
grapes to mellowed maturity,
the smoothest wine.

Aging
is the warm blood
held in the weighty goblet of body.

Aging
is all that is learned,
earned
and shed.

Aging
is the ancient relics
housing hidden birthplaces
in sacred spaces—
the discovered and undiscovered.

Aging
is a museum of memories,
both strong and fragile,
demanding revisiting,
gently suggesting
exiting.

Aging
is an attic
scented with the rust of time
and the dusty decades of knowledge.

Aging
is a library;
rich mahogany shelves
that
topple with antique books
and the voice of words—
etched and echoing
in the deep grooves
of the beautifully aging,
aged soul.

Recipe

Perfectly imperfect,
and ever-evolving,
I am not a mistake.

I'm simply a recipe,
tweaked and improving.

I am not a dropped cake.

Go if You Must

Go
if you must,

but before we decide
it's all turned to rust

you should know
that

you were the raft,
the craft,
the capsize,
the crash;

the mossy soil
of planted dreams,
the rain that waters.
the sun that streams;

the massage of the surf.
on the gritty sand,
the volcano before the ash,
the fruit of the land.

You were
a crescent moon
looking down on me,
with its crooked smile.

You were my feverish
distant oasis;

a love child
grown wild.

You were
fireworks
exploding
in a star-dusted sky;

my wildest ambition,
every fail,
every try;

every poem,
every gasp,
every sob,
every laugh;

the hand
that I clasped
till our bitter goodbye.

You were the day
when it's at last put to bed
an unpromised tomorrow,
a book not yet read.

You were the severed
kite string
when we went to the park,

but love's day is over.

Look…

now it's dark.

Spirits in the Fire

Let us gather now

to throw the kindling of our collective losses

onto a communal bonfire

then watch in awe at how large it grows,

how high the flames reach to flicker

and lick a sky darkened by grief.

Let us warm our hands over it

while it is still small,

then let our hearts break more

and pour into the flames

while they dance and roar

as the souls released

upwards soar.

Let the heavens open

and cry with us

as a weighty rain

strikes like gravel

upon our pain,

until we can't distinguish

whether it's our tears or heaven's

extinguishing the inferno.

Then let us sit in the cooling ashes

hands singed and sooty

clasping each other's,

grateful for the marks love left upon us.

We are baptized in fire and water

and come up as new beings

at peace,

now at one

with those released

as smoke

which carries memories

and travels far

as embers smolder eternally.

Remembering

Grief is a deepening.
It is soil
sifted, then settled.

Dark and rich,
it welcomes and waits
for your seeds of memories to be planted,
where they will grow, always.

Grief asks to befriend you,
to borrow your tears for its thirst.
Grief knows you want to run
but implores you:
Stay.
Stay, please
and remember.

Lean into grief's arms
and its achingly rich depths.
Reach into the soil
that holds the precious,
perennial bulbs you've buried,
then wait.

Love will grow
in its safe, dark secrets,
in ever-fertile gardens of mystery.

Grief is pressed into that soft deep dust
of humanity,
of friendship rare,

beautiful,
and forever alive.

Raw Silk

She is woven
from
and back into
raw silk:
imperfect,
pure of heart
but impure thought—

a product
of nature,
a spotted banana,
a bruised apple.

The bruised parts
are sweetest...

Durable thickness
brings warmth;
an army blanket,
a burlap sack
for strength,
a camping tarp
for survival,
resilience.

Raw silk doesn't
tear as easily
and isn't meant to be
slippery smooth
against naked skin.

And no horse
ever complained of
its
decidedly
burly
blanket—

slubs,
nubs,
and the variegated
color
disturbances,
she apologized for—

before realizing,
finally:
she is in fact
crushed velvet—

the heavy, timeless
drape;
weighty,
comforting
and luxurious
in its ageless,
antiqued
appeal.

This is how she feels:
like the discounted,
dented can—
perhaps undesired
but still useful,
capable of
nourishing.

The deliberate flaw
sewn into
the quilt
for humility;

burnished gold
gleaming its
caramel-hued warmth.

It didn't start that way...

There was fire
to be tried in
rusted sheen
in full potential
needing attention,

Just
rub
over time
and watch her shine.

She takes herself in,
gives herself a home,
makes herself
her own
yard-sale
treasure.

She becomes her own tailor,
a sculptress,
an artist, abstract
ironsmith,
farrier;

she was tarnished
and unfinished,

She didn't find
and take
and make
something
perfect.

As raw silk
she was perfect—
and as new as
a halo polished

under a steady,
careful,
almost holy
hand.

The Best Walk

Let us remove our shoes
as I walk you through a poem,
a hand-holding journey,
a short walk or long.

Maybe we'll tread in silence,
perhaps break out in song—

I think our muses and angels
have also come along…

See the signposts,
and the marks on the trees?
They point to feelings,
the perfect phrase,
a sort of praise,
a secret told in
whispering leaves.

And the weather
for our meandering mood
is perfect—
in fact, sublime.

Prose as worn footpaths
in rhyme
and metaphor as a map
you see,
are chosen from a place of longing
and imagination to be

explorers of the unexamined
following clouds
and birds
which point the way.

Did you bring a compass?
No?
That's good!
Let's see where words lead us
let's hear what the wind has to say…

Ah, a clearing
where we'll sit for a while
recite verses,
release pent-up tears
and then smile.

Having traveled far from intellect,
not anxiously looking behind,
poetry is a sojourn of heart and soul
so much more than mind.

Linear thinking is not part of our trip
The destination is found
through nature, the script
and lyrics discovered
creating space
for friends and for lovers.

And isn't it magical—
to go to another place
simply from reading the poem
in the lines on a face

and then, perhaps,
share
one of your own?

Come, the rain of inspiration is falling!

it's time
to head back home...

Ghosted

When I was ghosted,
I thanked the phantom who taught me
in hollow silence
what was fantasy,
when I thought it could
be real
this time.

I, in my way,
respected the specter
of what I once thought
"was."

Now just the cold unfeeling wisp
which never kissed my wistful lips

or touched my wishful thinking
when I had imagined
that our minds met,

when I fell through
a love shaped cloud
and found there was no net.

I wished this apparition well
as it dissipated from my past,

for ghosts float only into their own future.

In fleshly form don't last.

I gracefully allowed
those moody clouds
that obscured my dreams
to drift into memory,

though they gifted me but briefly.

And I felt only the slightest remnant
of sadness
and regret.

The vapor of vulnerability
and foolish trust,
I'd soon forget,

You had to go
and I ceased to question—
but simply
waved you away.

Ennui

Today was rough,
(I said was, not is)
for I have already fast forwarded to evening—
to the safety of my enchanted fortress.

I have detached from the moment
I am supposed to embody.

In this moment,
right now,
I'm observing the rain
crying down the windows of my car.

I don't cry as much as I'd like
or probably need to,
so I'm letting the sky do it for me.

"Why was today rough?"
I ask myself.

Outside forces
seem to be pushing me
back into my cocoon

my reactions do, too
as I am taunted by inner enemies
with their sneering voices.

I sit for several moments more
before emerging.

I feel the rain on my bare shoulders—
a cold caress.

I didn't dress
for this weather today…

Yesterday I was warm,
at home
in myself
and in my garden—

the sun,
a welcome massage on my skin,

As I inhaled the beauty
of flowers,
birdsong,
and approaching rain.

Today I feel a poignant aloneness
not akin to solitude
or loneliness.

I try to translate this language
of a vague sadness—
too tired for anger.

I try to ride it out,
these energy dips,
these mood swings
that exist
to forge my faith,
to hone my authenticity.

I am both sharp and soft
on any given day.

I put on a smile and fake it,
then wait for the end of my shift:
looking forward to evening:

purring,
candles,
tea,
writing.

Pining for the 'was' of this day
not this interminable
is.

Child's Sun

What did I do
to deserve a day
dawning such as this one—

bursting at seams
which stitch night to morning
with secrets to tell
and promises to keep?

The sun seems especially kind today
with its warm smile
like a child's idea of it;
an exuberantly scribbled drawing—
yellow and orange squiggles
for rays

a benevolent being
who lives in the sky
whose flaming light
so generously zig zags
and dances through trees,
dappling early summer leaves.

And as if that isn't enough,
throws twinkling diamonds
with wild abandon
upon the lake's
rippling surface
and tiny whitecaps
the wind creates
have a sound—

surely that of children
giggling.

The sun is
a dear friend visiting,
a whole day full of blessings
in its arms,
lingering until late afternoon
when longer shadows
arrive
waiting to welcome the moon

then it graciously
takes its sweet time saying "so long"
with the warmest of lingering embraces
and kisses upon heated skin,
until tomorrow...

Whoosh

The muse assumed
the soft
yet strong
voice of the Stoic
when today she queried me:

What if I told you
you could have a day
with no shame,
no fighting stance,
no tight shrug
of your shoulders?

Who might you be?

What if I told you that
for the next 24 hours,
you could choose to embody
total
utter
self-acceptance,
self-awareness,

be immune
to the voice of criticism
towards yourself
and others?

What if you knew
and felt
unequivocally

that you could safely
open yourself
to the possibility
of your own innate capacity

so that you could live
move
exist
be free?

What if you lived
like the center of the sun—
rays stretching outward
afraid of nothing
and no one?

Could you then behold
what your soul
already knows;

to cooperate with the seasons
to exist unquestioning
to be in no competition
with your fellow human beings?

What if I asked you,
begged you
to release your fear
to the clear air?

Who might you be?

Be that today
and see what happens…

you will fill the universe
with the relief
of your exhalation.

Places

When I told you I like poetry,
I read poetry,
I write poetry,
and even
had the audacity
(gasp!)
to refer to myself as Poet,

you smiled.

I saw in your face the image
that might have sprung to mind:

A young girl in a sundress,
skirt flowing over tanned legs
sitting in a field of daisies
on a sun-soaked day,
notebook
opened and waiting
on her lap.

Well,
I suppose
it can be that...
a perfect image of poetry
in its purity.

But you must also know
of the three a.m.
tear stung prose:

poems written
in a drunken, depressed stupor
my mind like a shorted-out circuit board,
sparks everywhere.

I just kept pouring fuel back then,
thinking that
my throbbing solitude
would turn into a soft fizzle
then fall into blissful, black silence.

That's not how fires and liquor works.
It made everything worse.
So much worse.

But oh yes—
best believe I still wrote,
practically illegibly,
but I've saved every note.

Looking out at the rain
through grimy window-panes,
I demanded solutions to problems
from pigeons, of all things.

I noticed the iridescence on their wings
and wondered why they're called filthy.
Why are they misunderstood?

I asked them if they were homing,
as they flew away
to yet another rooftop,
hopping and clumsily fluttering
from place to place
as I have done.

I longed to be as free as them,
their only worry being
from which lap or hand
their next crumb might come.

I found poetry
in their peculiar,
pleasing.
cooing purr...

I found poetry in the rain.

And somehow,
someway,
answers came.

When I told you
poetry saved my life
and continues to,

which image comes to mind:
a flower-strewn meadow,
or a place of pain?

Poems can be found in pastoral places, yes...

but mostly in tears and rain.

A Voice More Distant

I look to the future
no longer vague
or nebulous

but mine now
to embrace,
to caress,

eyes open,
deep breath.

A fierce force
roaring,
roused from deep slumber.

The quiet patter of rain
but wait—

Do you hear thunder?

Yet a distant whimper, still
stirred by vision
and sheer will,
stirs embers to this present fire
fanning a flame of
dormant desire.

Fear,
in yesterday's trembling voice
echoes

from a canyon vast,
a lonely past
(no choice)

whispering:

Please don't forget about me.
These links in the chain now broken,

are part of what set you free.

Poet's Nest

I don't waste moments
worrying about writer's block.

The muse is simply at rest—
a small brown bird,
a sparrow,
safely in her nest.

She just needs naps,
short or long,
then awakens ready to sing
a sweet kind of battle song.

After her time
of still observation,
she breaks her fast,
tasting the morning
on the tip of her tiny tongue—
the drop of ink
spilled from my quill.

Then words flow
into the day,
claiming it,
seizing the senses,
eagerly feasting.

But first...
the quiet mind,
the cave of night
from which she emerges,

refreshed,
wings outstretched
and ready to take flight
into that which I,
newly inspired,
write.

Sunflowers

I tend to them,
and watch them grow.

Actually…no.

They tend very much to themselves,
needing only the attentions of bees—
those suitors in their black-and-yellow best,
sowers of their future selves.

These daughters of the sun
turn up their haughty heads to face
their master,
stout, showy petals swept to the side
like the yellowest blonde tresses
of some insouciant dark-freckled maiden
tall and lusty—

presenting themselves on golden platters
of sudden and furious growth
before they grow too glorious,
too vain,
top heavy from the weight of their own
aspirations
for constant light,
for heat.

They weary and topple—
spent.

Then, new and younger blooms
around them
burst around—
they abound

while these older girls,
sun-sisters
with now bowed heads

cry their tears
of small dark seeds
which give birth to new life,

ensuring the cycle
the yellow flaming circle.

Their day in the sun,
each one has well-earned,

and when the season is done,

their lessons, I learn.

Grief Comes to the Garden

Death touches
our hard and soft edges,
both
as a tough, ropey stalk
supports the tender bloom,
so is death the part of life
uncelebrated.

A mighty presence
which wrests reaction
doesn't demand attention
yet won't be ignored—

death brushes up against us,
uninvited
and so rudely,
never even uttering a mumbled
"excuse me."

Death is a transition,
not an ending
and is not as strong
as Love.

Death doesn't expect
to be understood,
only accepted

as life's kaleidoscope
seen through a prism of tears.

Death remains a testament
to life's beautiful,
flower-like fragility
and the stem's strength
to endure the storms of grief,

even as our smoothest leaves
are stripped off
by the storm

seeming to disappear
with the wind
that scatters the seeds of eternity.

We were gifted the backbone to stand
straight and tall,
though the soul is stooped
when others need our stalwart support,

and the trust that a heart shattered,
as it crumples under the weight of sorrow,
will feel the the presence
of a mysterious universe,
cupping its hands
to gently catch our petals
and blow them back to us.

Guitar Stranger

As I rushed to work,
my short commute
around a charming lake—

to my left,
just then
a group of old men
fishing
off the dock
retired or
off the clock
full of talk
and laughter

sitting
on folded chairs
sipping coffee
in cardboard cups
forming an informal
portrait
of companionship.

Also noted,
around the bend;
a man
on a bench
guitar in his hands—
unrushed,
unhurried,
unworried.

This lovely lake surrounds
the island
of myself,
marooned in my own mind
until the noticing
this morning:

a lone man singing
or simply strumming,
composing a song?
Maybe he was humming,
inspired
by gentle water.

I wondered if he'd been there long?

The liquid lapis
lapped the sand
stretching out under
the canvas
of a cloudless autumn sky.

Perhaps the tune
was a simple, comic song;
an ode
to a love lost to summer
as autumn
ages the trees,
and days aren't quite as long.

Was it a poem set to music
as all songs really are,
the mystery of the universe found
in the strings of his guitar?

It could have been
the song of another he played.

My imagination suggests
a love song,
a lullaby,
a lonely lake serenade—

with swans,
frogs,
and fish
beneath the surface
swimming free.

These are this stranger's companions,
nor am I alone,
for this image stays
with me.

The Night Birds Are Singing

The night birds are singing
well after dinnertime—
a serenade to the first soft sliver of moonlight
gracing the windowpane.
They had sent out an invitation,
But the evening arrived late
the only excuse being;
"It's Spring!"

The night birds are singing
a welcoming chorus
to dusk;
their soprano chirping
and watery warbling
fills the trees,
which fills the air,
which fills the sky
and me.

The night birds are singing
and suddenly, their music seems
as though
it was coming from within me
from a hollow place.

The night birds are singing
in the darkness of me

where I hide my songs.

Autumn Song

Fall out of
and into
the certain
sweet sadness of the season

when the wind chimes sing
in a different voice—
perhaps an octave lower.

Endings are but new beginnings
disguised in shades of amber and umber

scented with clove
and mulling spices.

Melancholy autumn,
sometimes misunderstood
yet always appreciated by Earth
who,
awaiting her long winter's slumber,
wraps herself
in a warm wool sweater of gold.

I May Have Forgotten

I may have forgotten
what a lover feels like:

the scent his hair holds
at the end of the day,
what it is to roll over
and curve like a comma
around a form,

half-asleep and warm.

I may have forgotten
the sweet intimacy
of spoons clinking in unison
as we stir cream into our coffee,
the only sound breaking the silence of pre-dawn,
before words start the day.

I may have forgotten
the tiny shynesses
when it is new
to walk around nude,
in the innocent audacity of Eden's
delighted
exposure.

I may have forgotten
making a bed,
subtle hollows in the center
where we lay.

I may or may not
have forgotten
about the fire-roar of passion,
but there are enough verses written
and songs sung about that…
and these feelings appear out of nowhere
and tend to vanish
just as fast.

But have I forgotten
coming home to someone
who lovingly asks;

How are you?
How was your day?
This was mine…

Rowboat at the Lake

A rowboat,
seemingly abandoned
to the season
sits,
quietly observing the lake in early February
like a gentleman seated on a bench,
silent as fresh snow
in the morning
before any living thing stirs.

I walk to the lip of the lake—
it looks like the edge of an oyster shell.
A specter seems to speak to me.
It's the lake,
her voice cracking,
crackling
like her once fluid form,
solid enough
for the lightest,
most careful footfall.
Like her,
I too feel split open—
seams straining beneath the weight
of my winter white coat.
The dust of dawn flurries
rise up like tiny ghosts,
and in the darkness beneath her
a sort of dying peers upward,
still swirling.

Gulls
once milky

now gray against the snow
hover,
straddling the divide between solemn solidity
and what glistens and dances on the ledge.

Fat Canadian geese waddle insolently.
How wonderful to both fly and float
and wrestle over scraps of food
fallen on the boat.

Ambivalence hums just beneath my surface,
as well
where feelings skate like reckless children
precariously close
to the end of safety,
heaven flirting with hell.

Perhaps these birds dream of warmth
though hope is fragile as a feather—
winged ones
don't worry about things
such as weather.

They do adapt, after all.
The ones who stay behind
adjust their bodies,
backs,
and wings
to the threat of more snow
and the promise of spring.

Sorghum and cattails whisper to the
wind
scattering crystalline retorts
as it blows.

I tossed a smooth stone
across the rough surface,
to see which way it would go,
its gray heft skidding across the surface
performing a clumsy dance
as it found the divots.

Then the lake
sighed and started to sing
as she slowly swelled with silver.

Listen
she is singing more softly now—
a mother
gently imploring her children
to bravely accept winter's embrace
reminding them
as they shiver
of the promise that shimmers
just beneath her.

My lungs
and the day
fill with chillier air,
so I take my leave
of this icy reverie
and bid farewell
to the silent stalwart fellow

the rowboat
ready for his evening watch.

Gaia meets Venus

Fortunately,
I have never fallen in love
just once.

I may not have ever fallen in love
organically,
authentically,
as I move through this world,
this life
looking for it.

Sure,
I have fallen
in obsession,
in lust,
even in awe.

I've fallen down
the rabbit hole of desperation
for a him—
any him or them
to see me,

believing the consummate
lie
of validation.

But here is what
I now thankfully know;

I fall in love several times

a day
at least
with a leaf,
a crawling creature
really, any beast

or a round brown river rock,
the lace
of a spiderweb
so meticulously made.

I feel the arms of Gaia, the Goddess
embracing me—
when branches move and shiver
as the wind kisses a tree.

How blessed am I
to have various muses
who move me so deeply
with their subtle,
whispered voices
of inspiration,

that I discover a passionate
infatuation
with the art of
all creation—

its poems
and lyrics inscribed
in the lines and cracks
of the paths
I walk along,

in love with the sweetness
of solitude
which never feels
alone.

Child Mind

Thank you, child-mind
made of wonder,
made to wander
back to my center

from which the future
stretches out like rays,
like petals,
like arms.

Thank you, child mind
for still trusting,
for staying curious,

for taking
my aging hand
to walk with me through
the garden of
my life.

Morning With the Muse

Some mornings,
I don't expect
to awaken
in a clement mood.

I'm amazed at how much ache
asserts itself
in a body
doing nothing during dark hours.

Perhaps the muscles
so tight
as I exit the night
are the result of the running I do in dreams;
running to,
fleeing from.

It's strenuous to wrestle
with these
subconscious demons.

So I stretch,
shake the nocturnal voices
from my groggy head

and try to free the kite string of morning
from my clenched fist.

(Who wants to greet the day
with a clenched fist?)

Coffee flows.
Imagination follows.
Then I can write from the heart.

Words are found
in cob-webbed corners,
before the day even starts.

Before any noise is louder
than the songbirds tuning up.

A garbage truck still distant,
the coffee maker growling
or the cats—
restless for their breakfast;
talking,
purring,
meowing.

My mind still a bit sleep-fogged,
but creativity wants to greet the sun
with lyrics written
while visiting the moon.

The whisper that sits beside me
in this tiny cottage kitchen
is that of the muse.

I smile and ask her
how she takes her coffee.

Over-Sensitive

As a child,
I was chided:

Don't be so over-sensitive,
have a thicker skin.

No.

I don't want thicker skin.
I don't aspire to
toughen up.

I don't care to wear
the spiny casing of a crocodile
or an armadillo's corrugated shell.

The gray-green color
of a grenade
never suited my complexion
very well.

I want to wander through this life
yielding,

I don't wish to snap
and explode.

when treading through
the minefields of life,
I want to be exposed.

I want my skin to be
thinner and thinner
and
thinner still—

softer than
the wistful whisper
of a virgin's bridal veil.

Soft as the dust
on the wing of a moth,

soft as sea foam
or cappuccino froth.

Gentle as the sound
when a shy child sings

hushed as the velvet heartbeat
of a rosebud
opening.

I want to be the spiderweb
spun trustingly
in the crook of a windmill's arm;

the fragile membrane
which lines an eggshell—
so delicate
when unharmed.

I want to be
like a ripe peach—
easy to be bruised,

gossamer sheer
as if my soul was draped
in red tissue of crepe,
willing
to tear
when used.

I want to be
a heartbroken tear
coursing down the cheek
of the abandoned
and bereaved...

or upon the face
of a newborn infant,
when the womb it's ready to leave—

whose tender
feet will have
not yet touched

this calloused,
insensitive
world.

Greetings

Greetings from the void,

the place from which

a quiet voice is heard;

a child's whisper
in the midst of cacophony.

Greetings from secrets
that hold the disclosure,
from questions
which clutch
hidden answers.

Greetings from the canyon
of isolation
that echoes
the wistful song
of a hopeful lover
and their soft longing.

Greetings from a cloudless sky,
expanding
for one starling
who is not lonely
but content to fly freely…

to just be.

Its wings lifted by
the certainty of grace.

Greetings from this place:
The mirror
of a still lake,
which holds the clouds
in its wide embrace.

Greetings from the shadow
of long ago,
from a past
softened by time.

Greetings from the horizon
that remembers
yesterday
and releases tomorrow's sunrise
in today's mottled sky.

Greetings from the future,
gleaming like a palace imagined,
polished by years of pain

Greetings from the golden altar
of the unknown
wet and shiny with rain
and the promise of all that is yet to come.

Greetings from the armlike rays
of the ever beckoning sun.

Bedtime Stories for the World

I'd like to read a bedtime story to the whole world.

I'd like to,
in a soft soothing way,
calm the inner child in each and every soul.

We are all troubled.

But I'd like to be the one
who recites old-time rhymes
in a nurturing voice.

I'd like these inner children
to climb up on my lap;
to snuggle and lean in close—
so close I can feel their warm breath
as bodies relax.

And then I'd read a story
from the thick pages still unfolding—
a true tale of how we are slaying
three fearsome invisible dragons
called Defeat, Despair, and Death;

how mighty warriors
are lifting up their swords of faith
and shields of hope;
how the love of helping others
scoops up the world
in its sheltering wings.

I'd love to hum and sing lullabies
to the whole world right now,
not just at night,
but always.

I'd love to hear the children
who reside in everyone to chime in;
all the magical songs and sweet hymns
retrieved from the safe pockets
of memory's youth.

I'd love for the poets of now and of then
to rouse courage with words of valor
and turns of phrase
that cause a gasp,
a tear,
and a recognition of feeling.

I want the timeless stories
of *The Secret Garden,*
The Velveteen Rabbit
and *The Little Prince*
to summon comfort and courage—

while the wisdom of Hafiz, Rumi,
and Neruda
keeps us believing in the quiet bravery
of the innermost life,
to trust in the steady heartbeat of nature
revered by Oliver, Hirshfield, and Whyte.

I want to hear the angelic choir
of the voices of poetry
hushing these, our fretful children.

I want the world to be mesmerized,
to relax its shoulders,
as I gently turn the more delicate,
Bible-thin pages,
and whisper
hush…

I want *Goodnight Moon*
to cause eyelids to grow leaden,
warm milk for restless imaginings,
as the flames of the day's clanging fears
turn into the cool ash of twilight
as dusk graciously asks a dream to dance

so that all of Earth's children,
every last one
may sleep deeply
in sweet peace at last.

A Weed's Wishes

This innocuous bit of

snowy white fluff

stopped me

in my tracks.

As usual,
I had been distracted,
going about my life.

How have I not been noticing
what's all around
nearly crushed
under my careless foot?

I would have felt sorry
had I broken it…

Something humble in me
would have bent
to apologize.

But it's intact,
exquisitely so,
and poised
with potential energy.

What is this elderly dandelion
trying to tell me?

It must have lived
its fair share of wisdom
to have hair so white
and wispy.

Haven't I felt almost crushed at times,

my petals folded up
long enough?

What can I learn from this wishful weed
which waits for its seeds
to be lifted
by a shift in wind
to scatter itself far and wide?

I came upon this wildflower today,
and now I think I know why.

But I'll inquire again
of this fragile friend
about the mystery of waiting,
the beauty of creating

from this simple star
in a galaxy
of newly mown green;

a studded full moon
often unseen

full of promise,
this silvery sphere

not unlike the planet
so exquisitely near—

its fellows,
still yellow,
orbit around it.

They're a bit wilted,
not yet proudly
rounded.

But this blowball
stands ready
to release its gifts
upon the gentle breath
of a summer breeze.

I had my answer,
my heart swelling
as I blew
and closed my eyes,

affirming out loud
to the Universe:

so am I,
so am I,
so am I.

Unsung Songs

And what of the stanzas we never sing?
Where do the notes go?

Have they been dismissed
by the bandleader of intellect
with an imperious wave of his baton?

In the meantime,
morals and principles
line up outside
with pointed sticks

while feelings peek outside
from behind curtains
scandalously sheer

and their songs just want to be sung.

Art Let Me Know

Art let me know
it wants to,
it needs to
be part of life
be in life
be life.

Art let me know
it lives in love,
is in love
with the wild,
words of poetry,

in love with the hurricane
of your most recent heartbreak.

Art let me know
it longs to enter
abandoned buildings
in dirty cities

to transform scars into calligraphy
across the canvas of flesh.

Art let me know
in a whispered secret
that it wants to kiss me in watercolor,
and turn my briny tears
to pastel droplets,
like candy melted
when held in warm hands.

Art let me know
it wants to
finger-paint on my soul
with childlike abandon;

to take
reluctant fingers
and soften them
to hold the brush,
the microphone,
the pen.

Art implored me
to write,
to recite,
to sing,

to paint the world with
wild words.

Red Flags

Not only did I ignore them,
I also adorned them;
with sequins
and glitter,
then watched
them shimmer

as the sunshine
blinded my eyes.

Then I thought
to bleach them
to pastel pink,
a color soft
and harmless.

I gathered up a dozen blood-red flags,
arranged them in a vase
and celebrated
this Valentine's bouquet.

I fashioned a scarf from them
in futile hopes
of warmth.

I used them as sails,
seafaring wings
by which to fly
into a sunset
painted with
unrealistic expectations,

the wind of optimism at my back.
They often tangled,
these flags,
tightening
around my neck
as I stubbornly insisted they were anything
but
fiery
fabric
flares.

Or perhaps they were prayer flags,
crimson supplications
for all I wanted,
needed,
craved.

Or maybe
tribal symbols
of tolerance
and stoic strength.

Never was I willing
to see banners
defining and surrounding
unsafe boundaries:
Warning!
Hazard!
Danger ahead!

Ruby is the color
waved before an exhausted bull,
inciting its frenzied rage
before it falls...
panting,

bleeding,
dying.
Red flags
flapping
in the wind
full staff,

signaling storms
of uncertain origin
and the inevitable end.

Red flags
snapping angrily
at my choice
to turn a cheek
to certain consequence

to cover my ears
to the responsible voice
and the predictable fruition
of foolishness.

Wealth

Mostly, I wear silver;
I like its gleaming.

I like things that sparkle and shimmer,
like winter.

But gold glows.
Gold is warmth.

Fire is gold.

Rose gold is the color
when the sun retreats from the sky
on a late afternoon in autumn.

And once upon what feels like
a lifetime ago,
I sold all my gold—
ransomed everything precious to my soul
for amber elixirs
promising
the lie of warmth.

Halos are gold,
forged in the fires of life,

as well as leaves,
falling like coins
caught in shafts of sunlight.

I saw a play last week.
Silver signified the payment to Judas,
the fee for his betrayal.
Golden glitter was Christ's blood
shed.

Some of it sparkled on me.

But this morning was silver,
crystalline sterling frost
and icicles
formed by paralyzed tears.

Still, in that bitingly
bitter cold,
I spotted
a small, slender fox.

This evening I saw another,
then another—
their coats,
the color of rusted pennies.

Earlier, I thought of wealth
and found it
in vaults and treasure chests
all around me.

Today I am rich
in silver
and copper
and gold.

Souldust Reprise

Confetti that glimmers,
feathers,
and dirt;

the tumbleweed stuff
of hopes,
dreams,
and hurts;

stardust detritus,
the crushed shells of time,
sandgrains of memory,
gold unrefined—

all brushed off
as mundane,
these contents of days—

shards of rough glass
paving the way.

Birdseed strewn
without a care
the dander of cats,

a few stray hairs;

fibers and lint
found on the sheets,
dust mites
and pebbles,
crumbs that we eat;

atoms,
ash,
and cinders
comprise souldust
we've made.

The cells of mere body
is all that will fade.

Dandelion fluff
and cornsilk—
blown by fate's last breath,

time is measured
as present
and past

birth
and life
and death.

But come what might
and come what may,
the sun rests
at the feet
of dusk's
end of day.

And the heart knows
no time,
no rot,
no decay.

We're souldust,
life's glitter

the Potter's crushed clay.

Acknowledgments

souldust is my firstborn book; a true labor of love which has been gestating and kicking under my ribs for many years.

The author wishes to acknowledge the following, who helped to make the birth of this book possible.

My deepest gratitude to:

The benevolent universe, for its always faithful, ever-unfolding guidance.

To Beth, for her artistic skill in turning my abstract vision into beautiful cover art.

To Eva, my editor at Fiverr, for her meticulous attention to detail and gracious encouragement.

To the many creative writing mentors and workshop leaders who over the years, helped me realize the depths of my creativity.

To the muses in nature who inspire me daily.

To every trauma-turned-learning experience which honed my empathy and sensitivity to fellow strugglers and survivors.

To my Facebook friends and fellow poets, who became my chosen family, especially Carolyn.

To Carol and Stephen, who have always had my back.

To all living and departed poets who inspire me and shine like beacons, continually lighting the way.

To Joni Mitchell and Trevor Hall, whose musical art provided the soundtrack as I wrote every day.

To the voice within me which grew louder and bolder than the external ones of my past, the more I learned to believe in myself.

To my dear children, who always assured me that my dreams and aspirations to become an author would indeed become a reality one day.

To Alice, who made sure this book would look perfectly polished.

Most of all, I acknowledge Poetry itself; the gift of words, which I truly believe can heal a wounded world. *La Poesia e Vita.*

With all my love, Lisa

About the Author

LISA O'NEIL GUERCI hails originally from Boston, but has lived in New York State since 1996.

A mother of two adult children and "Gigi" to two grandsons, Lisa is employed as a professional personal care assistant and advocate within the elderly community—a job to which she is devoted and finds great personal fulfillment in.

When not working, Lisa enjoys spending time with family, writing, reading, listening to music, cooking, gardening, and traveling all over the world... in her mind.

Lisa has also dabbled in the field of freelance photojournalism for local newspapers, and finds endless inspiration in capturing art with her camera. Living by a lake has proven as well to be a source of inspiration, creativity, and imagination.

Lisa's poetry has appeared in a handful on online publications, one piece included in an anthology entitled *Blue Motel Rooms: The Art and Poetry of Joni Mitchell*, available on Amazon. Her work was recently included as one of the "Poets of the World" in *World Healing, World Peace 2024*, an anthology published by Inner Child Press.

Having only a small circle of "in real life" friends, Lisa attempts to limit her time on social media, but nearly always fails. She has also managed to become an unapologetic "cat lady," and considers her twin Hemingway housemates to be pudgy little people in furry gray suits.

Sharing a deep affinity for birds, Lisa has "parented" parakeets since childhood; their voices providing a kind of background soundtrack to her days.

Poetry is the enduring passion of Lisa's non-linear life, and she writes in some capacity every day. She has volunteered her time to Confetti Magazine as a poetry selector and taken part in various writing workshops and courses over the years, as well as participated in retreats in and around the Tri-state area. She has twice been a featured performance poet at the Stark Reality open mic in New York City, as well as in Confetti online Magazine.

Lisa was honored last year to have been selected to read her poem, "Still a Beautiful Sky" at a 9/11 memorial ceremony in Somers, NY.

She greatly enjoys being an active member of communities of like-minded people within the creative arena, and is an adept cook; taking delight in trying new recipes, and testing them out on appreciative family members and friends.

Lisa currently resides in a quaint lakeside cottage in Carmel, New York, where she loves being outdoors honing her photography skills, and is diligently at work on a memoir detailing her experiences in the cult she was raised in and heroically escaped with her young daughter in 1992.

She is also engrossed in the project of compiling and categorizing the many poems from her sizable collection for future publication.

souldust is her first book.

www.ingramcontent.com/pod-product-compliance
Lightning Source LLC
Chambersburg PA
CBHW020906100426
42737CB00044B/495